Forward Movement Publications
412 Sycamore Street
Cincinnati, Ohio 45202